TRINITY GUILDHALL

Sound at Sight

Piano

book 2

Grades 3-5

Published by
Trinity College London
89 Albert Embankment
London SE1 7TP UK

T +44 (0)20 7820 6100
F +44 (0)20 7820 6161
E music@trinityguildhall.co.uk
www.trinityguildhall.co.uk

Printed in England by Halstan & Co. Ltd, Amersham, Bucks.

Sound at sight

Playing or singing music that has not been seen before is a necessary part of any musician's life, and the exploration of a new piece should be an enjoyable and stimulating process.

Reading music requires two main things: first, the ability to grasp the meaning of music notation on the page; second, the ability to convert sight into sound and perform the piece. This involves imagining the sound of the music before playing it. This in turn implies familiarity with intervals, chord shapes, rhythmic patterns and textures. The material in this series will help pianists to develop their skills and build confidence.

Plenty of pieces are given throughout, but this is more than just a book of specimen tests. Guidance is given on new skills before they are incorporated in short pieces of music. This contributes to making this a thoroughly practical course in developing sight reading skills, whether it is used for examination preparation or to increase confidence in the context of solo playing or ensemble work.

Trinity's sight reading requirements are stepped progressively between Initial and Grade 8, with manageable increases in difficulty between each grade. Some tips on examination preparation are given at the back of the book. In all cases, however, references to examination tests are avoided until *after* the relevant material has been practised. This is deliberate: many pupils find the prospect of being tested on sight reading skills to be quite inhibiting at first. The aim is to perform new pieces—the fact that they may be examination tests as well is far less important.

Acknowledgements

Thanks are due to the many composers who have contributed to the series: James Burden, Humphrey Clucas, Colin Cowles, David Dawson, Sébastien Dédis, Peter Fribbins, David Gaukroger, Robin Hagues, Amy Harris, Peter Lawson, Jonathan Paxman, Danielle Perrett and Michael Zev Gordon.

Thanks are also due to Matthew Booth, Luise Horrocks, Geraint John, Joanna Leslie and Anne Smillie for their technical advice.

 The *udjat* symbol is an Egyptian hieroglyph called the 'sound eye', and was associated with the god Horus.

● Introduction

If you have worked through Book 1 in this series, you will be familiar with extensions and with changes of basic hand position. These are now used freely and you will need to plan these as you read through a new piece.

New keys open the way to greater variety. To start with, you will need to be familiar with majors up to one sharp or flat (which will increase to three sharps or flats by the end of the book) and A and D minors (E, B and G minor later on).

New textures are encountered here too, with free use of chords and simple part-playing.

● Chord-playing

At this stage you will also need to be able to play chords in either hand. Practise the following chord-shapes in different keys.

Thirds   Fifths   Triads

Fourths   Sixths

The '3-chord trick'

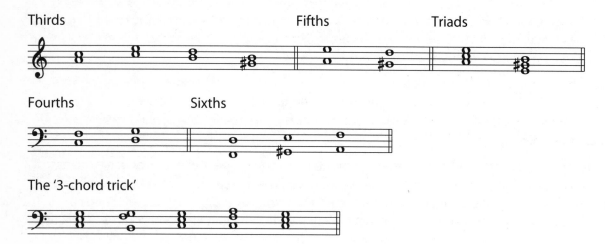

● Phrasing

Short phrases need clear definition from this level. On the piano, the first note of a slurred pair should be louder than the second note.

The same is often true in short runs or groups of notes. Rising groups, however, may need to get louder instead.

Rests are silences that must be observed. Do not hang on to the previous note!

• Dynamics and pace

Now **mp** is added to *f*, *p* and *mf*. If **mp** and **mf** occur together, **mp** should be slightly quieter.

Andante means flowing gently at a calm walking pace.

1   **Andante**

Now you are ready to play these pieces.

2   **Andante**

3   **Allegretto**

4 Moderato

5 Andante

6 Allegretto

Notice that this piece changes from minor to major.

7 **Moderato**

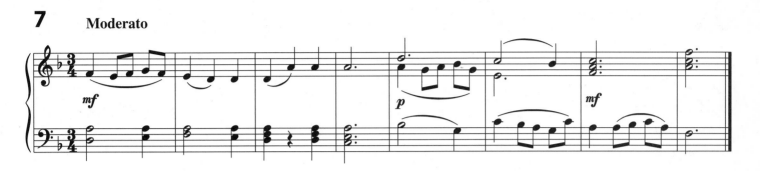

8 **Allegretto**

9 **Moderato**

10 **Andante**

11 **Moderato**

12 **Andante**

13 Allegretto

14 Moderato

15 Moderato

16 Moderato

17 Allegretto

18 Moderato

 Melodies 1–18 are of the standard used by Trinity for Grade 3 examinations.

• Introducing B♭ major

The new keys at this level include D major and E minor, but the most important one to cope with in playing at sight is B♭ major. Play the scale, hands separately and together, noticing the fingering. The feature to remember is that the thumb comes after a black key when travelling outwards from the centre of the piano, in either hand.

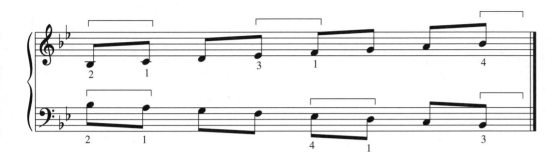

• Accidentals

Notes outside the key are introduced here. Accidentals apply for the whole bar, so be careful if the note appears more than once.

Practise moving a finger onto and off a black key without looking down. There should be no hesitation in finding the right key by feel alone.

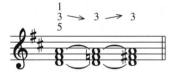

• Dynamics and articulation

Gradual changes of volume can be indicated by the words *cresc.* (*crescendo*) and *dim.* (*diminuendo*) or by 'hairpins':

This is quite easy in runs but will need more practice when there are leaps or chords involved. Listen carefully to make sure that the effect matches your intention.

Do not overlook *staccato* (short, detached) or accented notes amongst *legato* (smoothly connected) ones: they must be clearly articulated.

• Dotted rhythms

You have already seen dotted minims but now you will encounter dotted crotchets. These will almost always be followed by a quaver (♩. ♪). If the other hand has crotchets, this rhythm will pose few problems, but if the other hand is sustained (as in melody no. 19), make sure that the dotted note is not shortened: feel the pulse strongly, as if the passage were written with a tied crotchet (♩͡♫).

19 **Andante**

20 **Allegretto**

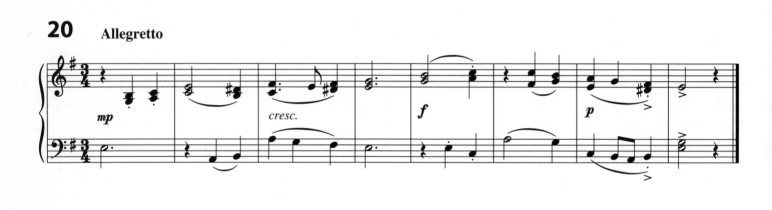

21 **Allegretto**

22 **Moderato**

The next piece uses more than one line (or system). It is very important to read ahead so that there is no hesitation at the end of the first system as you find your place.

23 **Andante**

24 **Moderato**

25 Allegretto

26 Moderato

27 Andante

28 Andante

29 Moderato

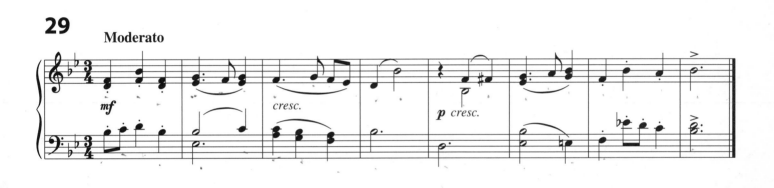

30 Allegretto

31 **Moderato**

32 **Andante**

33 **Moderato**

34 **Andante**

35 **Moderato**

 Melodies 19–35 are of the standard used by Trinity for Grade 4 examinations.

• New keys

The new keys and this stage are A and E♭ major, B and G minor.

Remember that in E♭ major, as with other flat keys, the thumb comes after black notes when moving outwards from the centre. This will help you when planning fingering.

In B minor, remember that the left hand starts (unusually) on 4th finger.

• A new time signature

$\frac{6}{8}$ should be felt as two slowish beats in the bar, each one subdivided in three. The beat is a dotted crotchet.

You will also need to be able to subdivide the beat into semiquavers, whether the beat is a crotchet or a dotted crotchet. Practise these patterns in your head:

Take care that dotted rhythms involving semiquavers are neat and not 'lazy'. Think of the semiquaver here as being linked with the note that follows it rather than with the dotted note.

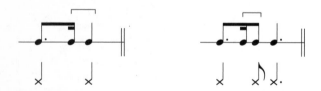

36 Moderato

As pieces get longer, there will be more variety of texture and style to cope with. Noticing the sequences (patterns of notes repeated at a different pitch) in the next piece will help you. Make sure that you execute the rhythm correctly.

Enjoy greatly the *rall.* in bar 7 and the pause in bar 8, and the similar moment at the end.

37 Andante

In the next piece, the harmony is very important. Ensure that you hold the lowest left-hand note for its full length.

Try to use the pedal, changing every bar with the change of harmony.

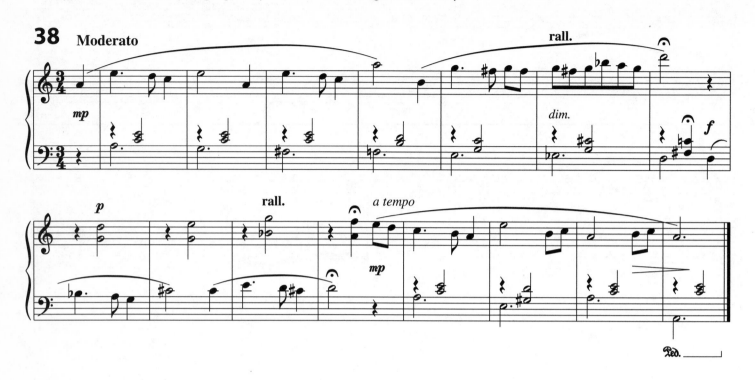

40 Maestoso

41 Andante

42 Andante

43 Andante

44 Moderato

45 Moderato

48 Andante

49 Moderato

50 Lento

51 Poco moderato

52 **Andante con moto**

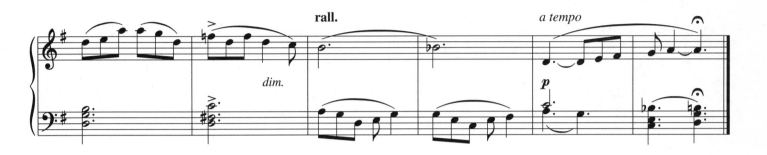

 Melodies 36–52 are of the standard used by Trinity for Grade 5 examinations.

• Examination preparation

In an examination, you have half a minute to prepare your performance of the sight reading test.

It is important to use this time wisely. First of all, notice the key and time signature. You might want to remind yourself of the scale and arpeggio, checking for signs of major or minor first. Look for any accidentals, particularly when they apply to more than one note in the bar, and plan changes of hand position.

Set the pace securely in your head and read through the test, imagining the sound under your fingers. It might help to sing part of the music or to clap or tap the rhythm but the most important thing is to get a clear idea of what the music will sound like. You can also try out any part of the test if you want to, although it is often a good idea not to do this until you have read through the piece first.

Have you imagined the effect of the dynamics? Do you need any pedal?

When the examiner asks you to play the piece, play it at the pace you have set. The rhythm is more important than anything else: make sure that this is accurate, whatever else is going on. If you make a little slip, do not try to go back and change it—the mistake has already gone. Make sure instead that the next thing is right.

Give a performance of the piece. If you can play the pieces in this book, you will be well prepared for examination sight reading, so enjoy the opportunity to play another piece that you did not know before.